Gallery Books
Editor Peter Fallon
THE SWERVE

Peter Sirr

THE SWERVE

Gallery Books

The Swerve
is first published
simultaneously in paperback
and in a clothbound edition
on 1 October 2023.

The Gallery Press
Loughcrew
Oldcastle
County Meath
Ireland

www.gallerypress.com

ISBN 978 1 91133 854 1 *paperback*
     978 1 91133 846 8 *clothbound*

A CIP catalogue record for this book
is available from the British Library.

The Swerve receives financial assistance
from the Arts Council of Ireland.

Contents

for Enda and Freya, as always,
and for Jack Wyley

A Saxon Primer

Más allá de este afán y de este verso
me aguarda inagotable el universo.
— Borges

Then I think of Borges going blind,
of what he said about the soul.
He was trying to understand
why a man who was losing the world
would seek out swords and monsters,
blunt-voiced Saxons in the mead hall.

It's that the soul must know it's immortal,
he said, and its hungry turning circle
takes everything in, achieves all that's possible.
There's a kind of secret knowledge
enfolds us, reaches everything we do,
or else all we do is the knowledge and the soul.

Beyond all this, the sweated grammar,
the effort to know one thing after another,
on the other side of the poem the universe is waiting,
patient and inexhaustible. Time and again
the light keeps fading from what we love
though we turn and turn to it, singing

to blunt the darkness, to fold the light back in.

Meanwhile

meanwhile February shoots up
in mimosa plumage
— Friederike Mayröcker

It's that nothing happens afterwards
or everything happens all the time.
The wind keeps pummelling the willows,
the gulls come to blows on the road.

Meanwhile the traffic crawls up the hill,
the mirror stares into the hall.
Meanwhile the aisles are crammed,
the new specials shine on the shelves.

Meanwhile the books are taken down
and someone measures the floor.
Meanwhile your bulbs have come up,
your clothes have dried on the line.

You're gone but: meanwhile your car reverses out
and a new life parks in the drive.
Meanwhile is where you live now
watching the clouds go by.

Meanwhile: apex of grammar,
the world's first gift and final promise.
Meanwhile: our one true place,
our home from home.

Meanwhile the airports are open,
the boats are approaching the shore.
Meanwhile the moon wakes up in the river
and leans back, a little further each time.

A Birth in Winter

Nasce um Deus. Outros morrem.
— Fernando Pessoa

One god is born. Another dies. Fields
and hedgerows slip through the light,
then press back, blinking; the holly
burns with the ivy now, yew tips
test the sky, taste the air. Children come
with frosted breath to the clearing
and set the trinkets in the crib. It is the night,
the big one when the god comes down,
when the old gods gather and retreat,
filling the trees with their breath,
leaving gifts of twigs and berries, snow
fingering the branches of the yew.
Or it is the morning after,
the windowsills empty, the birdmen
preparing their costumes, but for now
the day is undecided, the glasses undisturbed.
It is the morning, very early. The gods
are in their swaddling clothes, they sleep
in the world's tight grip, waiting for themselves.

Talking to the Birds

He described how a woman of the Boa tribe on the Andaman Islands who died in 2010 would, during her final years, 'speak a lot with birds because there was no one around to speak her language'.
— *New York Times*

When no one was left
who understood our language
I sat outside and talked to the birds

and when the birds went in
I talked to the moon, I sang to the stars.
When the rain came I told it a poem

and when in the morning the sun
spread across the floor
I danced from side to side with the broom,

pulling stories from my sleep,
telling the clock about my friends and relations,
how we sat all night by the fire

and played music and talked non-stop
without knowing we were using the language up,
that on the other side of every word

silence hid, waiting for its time.
Learn this language, I tell the birds,
and sing wherever you go

the wild ways we used it. By now
this house must surely have it, the grammar
long seeped into the furniture

and when I lay my hands on the table
I know the wood is listening
and the flowers when they open will say my name.

History

She slips through the open window, my secret cat,
arranges herself on my chair
as if she's always lived there.

I stroke her fur and touch the history
of every cat I've known or owned
or greeted as we passed each other by.

She's not mine and doesn't care.
I'm not hers and don't complain. She moves now,
stands on my desk, tail high, curious.

Behind her on the screen, stared at for an hour,
four young dogs huddled together
in first century Rome,

a woman's boot from Scythia
taken out of the frozen ground.
The Persians rose and fell,

maybe Alexander passed her by.
Someone, I hope, must have stopped
to wonder at the intricate, beautiful boot.

The cat doesn't care
that her tail is a millimetre
from palaeolithic dildos, a funerary boat

packed with rowers eager for the shore,
or she's purring her way back to Egypt
with her umpteen lives, her chain of fur

passed from hand to hand
down a well of time. The dogs have yet
to open their eyes; one marble blink

and they'll be here, dozy and hungry.
What news of the Achaemenids, cat,
what's blowing in from Persepolis,

what secrets from the tombs
as you unwrap the linen from your paws
and go on patrol among the mouse and bird souls

or sneak to the temple
to press your head against the brow
of the cat-headed goddess? History

bristles under the touch, the pages fly up,
the cities sink farther down.
Trimmed in tin, crystals of pyrite, gold foil,

its glass beads secured with sinew,
the boot lives on, the steps
survive. Touch it now and mew,

feel her fingers on your fur,
then stretch to nudge your head against mine.
We'll stay in some shadowed corner, watch

the ages slip by, all hungry eyes
and electric repose, and not
biding but hiding our time.

The Uncollected Animals

When they came for us we sank back in the scrub
until they gave up. When they were gone
we set out for their places, as if we might
snare the silence by snout or antler, counting by heart
the broken stairways and hollowed cathedrals.

We descended into the tunnels,
held conferences in the squares,
stepped aboard trams and nibbled at rails.
We lowered our voices and sang more sweetly
and the songs crossed the widening skies
though the lion still ravaged the lamb,
the owls still swooped on the mice and the wasps
went on stinging their eggs in the bellies of bugs.

Eventually, of course, they returned,
singly at first, wide-eyed and afraid,
then more came, with guns and knives,
leading skinny beasts in pairs
who looked at us and skittered and ran
or tried to, but were led back
and manhandled into makeshift pens.

Some of the men set up a table in the square
and one slit a spare throat and stood
in the blood drench spilling prayers.
We shrank back and made for the tunnels
and for once we came together, all of us,
and there in the dark decided

enough was enough. While they slept
we moved like a great tide through the streets
washing over barricades and altars.
We took their guns and woke them
and herded them the way they'd come.

In the outskirts we found it,
looming on the rocks near the reservoir,
empty but for one shivering dove. Softly,
we called to him and he dropped the branch
and came to us. Then we sent them
back up the gangplanks again
and stood a long time waiting for the rain.

River

The stone sits in the hand, still sharp.
Maybe we're never really lost.
They dig out more flint from the old riverbank.
How many millennia since the river moved?

A river of tools: axe and adze, a river of hands
using the tools. The struck wood flows through time,
the bone-worked joints hold up. And there we are,
standing on the riverbank busy as ever.

The tools accompany us, speak for us,
whatever we do flows on
like these thousands of axe heads the artist collected
and laid side by side, a field of stone

that must long to lift, that must include,
hovering overhead
or stretched taut to where the handles begin,
the roughened hands ready to strike again.

Border Control

Not everything I said I did
I did in fact. Not literally.
But if it wasn't all true
it was true-*ish*.

Some of us need
a little help.
Human Resources
can't find the file?
I'm human, I'm resourceful.

And which is better,
the given thing
or the lifted wing?

You think death
will be different?
Charon with his degrees
and testimonials, the fat dog
with his breeder's certificate

and all the aching,
scrutinized dead
stamped, waved
through, passed
from Billy to Jack
and Milly to Susan.

You think they're all
kosher? No angel ever
looked the other way?
No demon faked her fire?

Keep the stamps, the turnstiles,
hold my papers to the lamp,

that cost so much
and may still persuade.

And even if they fail
and the forged soul must stew
I'll keep whoever I am
to myself, whisper
to the dust or feathers
in the grey valleys

some bread
is better leavened,
some lies
deserve their heaven.

C in Old Age

How long have I been here, outliving myself?
Rome sinks behind its veils, the young poets flail
from bar to bar, their tongues on fire. Clodia,
I add you to my dictionary, you

would not like me now. Or did our trolleys bump
last week in the market? What was it I was looking for?
The bread was stale, the fish had travelled
almost as far as I had. *Salve, piscis* . . .

They go round and round composing
oceanics to set the libraries buzzing. Oh
but I had it, I was a very whale
among the boastful fry posting themselves

on the platforms. Self-pummelled
prince of hurt, begging for more,
wearing my heart on my bedsheets, relishing
the treacheries. Now the ants line up to hear

carmina of ordinary despair. We who lived after
drag our chairs into the sun and go over
how much we lost selling guns or coffee,
how many nights we spent clutching

the tattered blanket around a beloved shoulder.
The light, though, was irresistible
and the chair holds up in the broken yard.
I listen to my neighbour's piano and break out the wine,

fail to care the odes are singing in the drawer.
The wood listens, keeps its counsel.
Postcards come once a year
from places only the stamps remember . . .

Haunting School

Such joy at first you'll wonder
why you prized them so much, too solid earth
and lumbering flesh. That first night, though,

that first giddy thrill as you enter the house,
keep it close, as something you might fall back on;
remember always how it felt: released

from school, the tricks studied, all the old
conjury, orbs hovering, mists
and vapours, the creeping

into the edge of the photograph,
the shadow in the video, the smells
so distinctly us no one who knew could miss . . .

And there you are, passing though the wall
like an old hand, the same wall
who knows how often you touched or leaned against.

You touch your touch, you float, you graze,
you move from cheek to cheek and lip to lip,
you stray into the minds of those who knew you

and feel a kind of conversation flow. That smile,
that tiny gesture, that hint of a tear — it must be you!
And even when that goes and the faces are farther away —

so far that if one of them saw you standing there
with that eternal half smile, beyond the terror,
they'd scratch their heads to figure who you were —

you'd still hold to it, still feel the same self stir.
Then the slow, loving procession
into angel mode, unageing, watching

the future come, the breath tighten, the grip slacken
until the house is empty again.
No one remembers you now; it's time

to walk alone. The rooms are colder, the mirrors
harder. Up and down and in and out you go,
continually searching. You open a door, lift

a coverlet to meet a child's unseeing eyes,
you inspect the parents and shake your head,
you shake your unbody but if the smell

spills out no one seems to notice, you've sunk
into the furniture, you're lodged
like spiders, like old carpets, you're atmosphere.

This is the sulking time. You've seen the films:
you stamp and grumble, throw stuff around, dig up
tricks from the book that get the specialists out.

Maybe you oblige them, maybe not:
the real strop is you know no one on the planet.
This is ghost hell, the faces that have not repeated,

the voices unfamiliar, love sinking
through its endless ocean. What's the job then?
The dance of the lost in a summer garden,

a gleam no one can quite define. Flittings and rumours.
You flutter your wings and press towards the light.
You flutter your wings and long for the dark.

You follow the turning planet and try to step off.
Over and over the questions come:
What holds me here? Where did I go wrong?

Try to stay calm. Stand still in the corner
or huddle in the chandelier. Flap your skull and call
Ghostly Resources. Acknowledge your feelings, then
    move on.

The empty earth is your forever workplace.
Think of that first wall. Pass through like that again,
not a thing resisting, dust shining on your woken face.

Salt

A man moves through the rubble foraging for rainwater.
A woman enters the burning temple with her children.
Soldiers loading the treasures on trucks, every

last building razed. The silence of the streets,
bodies lying in the crushed market.
When everything is gone the cursing begins.

Think of Cato ending every speech
no matter what the subject —
Damn Lucius, the sanitation, those

Greek-loving stargazers — with *Carthago est delenda!*
Legend was they sowed the ground with salt
but that was Hattusa, that was Taidu, Arinna,

Hunusa, Irridu, and Susa, that was Abimelech
pouring salt into his own capital after the revolt.
The windows begin to shatter, the shrapnel

flies, a spill of water turns to ice on the floor
and the neighbours are dead in the courtyard.
Delenda, Branagan said, peering from his dais,

gerundive, see, feminine, from *Carthago*,
combining with the verb 'to be' to leave
nowhere to hide; no ifs and buts, it *must* be destroyed.

A whole week it took, retreating to the neighbouring villages
every evening for drinks and supplies.
After the dynamiting, the horses stabled in the churches.

The arguments, the colours, avenues robed
with trees and laughter. *Kill every man within a kilometre.*
Salt for the ground and the tongues of the slaughtered.

Days of the Dead

I woke up from that conversation with a dead friend
confused, anxious, not because of what we'd said,
which had been relaxed, lively — all the old ground,
how things connect, how poems remember poems,
how the more we go on the more there is to find —
but because afterwards I failed to find my way home,
lost my wife and daughter, missed the plane,
couldn't remember even the city's name.

The dead come back, you say, and this is exactly
the time of year they swell the air, sign
the thickening census of leaves or rain, lean
a little closer to desk or stair, or sit, raising
their glasses at the crowded table. And then
you tell me how the troubled one came to you,
the death still raw, how the white shirt
you lifted from the wardrobe blackened in your hands

as if ink had been flung in anger
from deep within. Shocked by the stain
you threw it in the machine but when it came out
it was pristine, whiter than it had ever been.
What does that mean? The dead return like Halloween
tricksters, bearing grudges and unhealable pain?
Your mother sat on the end of your bed and smiled,
a belovèd dog pawed his way in and barked again.

The angry and the eased share the place,
you light your candles and keep the peace.
I keep my dead in sleep and dreams,
unreliable haunters, scattered in the wood,
wandering the edges of nameless cities.
Or I stare at the page where I try to write them,
half listening for a sigh or whisper, some
slight disturbance in the room, all the time praying

whatever they are should keep its distance,
move with the blank insistence of wind or sun
or lie quiet and await its season. *Zad*,
the driver said, meaning the airport never found,
the one sure word returned. I nod
as I step aboard, as if I understand, as if unsurprised
death should have its own language, the book
always open, the rules all around.

Lines for My Daughter

One must remain untiringly alive, looking into the future and feeding on the living reserves which memory and oblivion together accumulate.
— Boris Pasternak, *Essay in Autobiography*

I could see you there, deep in the vertical wood,
watching the trees climb from floor to floor

or here, another future, this woman in the sun
sewing seedpods on her daughter's dress

as under the waves the saved fruits ripen.
Whatever happens we'll lodge in the cracks,

walk hand in hand in a diminished land?
Meteors could get here first, the ice run out

so all I'll say is *not this*, where the days close their fists
and press against the glass, not this deadly playlist.

Not the interval but the concert whole,
not the narrowing street but a city of wild paths

tangled, unextinguishable, not the shrinkage
where we count our steps but the giant stride

the heart
        untiringly alive.

May

*. . . I kept asking where you are, souls
of the dead.*
        — Adam Zagajewski

I'll look for you in a forest in May
along with the others, young and old,
forgotten and remembered, ghost poets
of ancient conferences reconvened in branches
where squirrels quarrel over metres
and mice read papers on closure. I'll stand
drenched in finches, rooks, blackbirds,
each of whose songs will have lines of yours
as the trees and sky will have your soul,
as my standing there, eyes on the deer,
hands on the bark, thoughts in the clouds
will have your smile, and everything in between,
everything around will still fall in
like a dawning notion, a voice hungry to open.

Totenlied

Where's the song for this? And who should sing it?
The houses saw us where once we wandered,
our witnesses the vanished floors, dust and water,
the baths running, the persistent grasses.
Or as if we should call up the hands that held us,
that lifted us up and set us down, rooms where we sat alone.
Childhood yet to be harmed, come to us and speak again . . .

Imagine if the years had parted then and you looked down
and, *what?*, waved a magic reversing wand? —
as if change were in our gift, second after second
of subtle alteration to call back the pain,
spooling the thread until you held it again.
The tables we shared, the hands that held us
that suffered their own breakages . . .
but nothing held you in the end.

The gift of the future is we can't climb over,
stare down from the wall at the dark garden
of what will come of us. It grows how it will,
wild and ungovernable, our only comfort

that its secrets hold, that no shady figure
creeps out to whisper in our ear
however close you hold these years or live
in the rooms' embrace the houses, the years
collapse, the grasses shake, the heavy hand
finds its way across and settles on your shoulder.

'We are gathered . . . '

We are gathered
around a photograph of you

some silences
beyond entering

some choices
beyond arguing

though helplessly
we'd argue it now

in the dark room
in the room

where your body
unplugged

flows in its own aftermath
breathing its last

some places
beyond escape

some nights
beyond ending

the dawning
stuck fast, as if

a world held back
or persuadable brightness

finally burned
beyond persuasion

and fell to ash

Light in June

I saw the shadows on your wall, the sun low, just
trees and pipework blown from themselves, throwing shapes
in the June evening on your garden wall and on the back
    of your house
as you sat inside eating, not seeing, not counting
how the dusk light played with your building
or pinked the brick near the corner. Most of what goes on
goes like the shadows across walls
unseen, the world shines beyond us.
Somewhere a treasure is clasped in a dying hand
and the things go on in their own lives,
the bone spoon lodged in a cavity, the dice
lying quiet in a roundhouse wall, holding for the wager
of light or stone or air, the day that will gather
everything waiting, everyone lost, and join them together
    again.

Second Take on 'Haunting School'

Those tricks and bumps, noises in the night,
faces in the bath water — you think
that's how it is? Dragged from your dreams
into unquiet corridors, ghouls in the mirrors.

The truth is much worse: we haunt
only ourselves, are our own
black terrors — it's our hair mostly
stands up in fright, our screams

assaulting the night. True,
we stare into your faces, and yes, your breath
streams across our palms, but we touch
not touching, speak without speaking, and you

whom repeatedly we badger lie unstirring
and never move or change direction.
We pray you wake, or at least imagine
one crooked glance in a million. The mirror

cracks at last, the room grows colder, hotter,
one perfect self-forgetting
where you put on your scariest suits,
sweep out of your lives and come for us . . .

Constructing the Memory

Now I am become death, the destroyer of worlds.
— J Robert Oppenheimer

Please, step back, go no further, you've come
far enough. You have to imagine
the place is language first —
the markings, the gargoyles,
the strangeness of the landscape all around
even if the speakers have disappeared
who should be here
handing the darkness down
from year to year.

There was incense, the moon streaming through
the aligned opening, the weight of ages
in surplice, chasuble, the fingers turning
the slow pages of the hymnal, listening
for the initiates to take up the tune.

No cathedrals or infinities:
this was the priesthood of the toxic grail,
hand after hand on a rotting scroll. Please
stand back. We would have preferred
flowers, the warm sun in the fields,
nights we sang till dawn.

Look for us instead
where the sky deepens above the megalith
and a sudden discordance unsettles the song.

To Whom . . .

Of course the skills may have vanished
or the language broken up, so many lumps
of indecipherable clay in the satellite library.

I stand here before you —
something: dust-messenger? Designated
sliver? Last person out, remember

the planet . . . I'm sorry,
the role was inexactly determined,
in such haste assigned and after all

I hardly expected the responsibility.
Still, this is what you have; what, really,
you always get. Open the box

and out shambles a minor functionary
with his bag of beans. This is how
we counted, these were the names of the kings.

Study the spreadsheets. I put down
what I could, kept adding slides to the deck.
Not everything would play. The technology

is brilliant until it isn't. Heat
the clay. Or not? Be patient.
This is us. We weren't. Or not enough.

The Messenger

is always wrong have you noticed
               I swear
I never touched the corpse I was nowhere near
I was watching the match in the security hut
then stopped off for shashlik
             see the stain on my shirt
             I almost didn't come
anticipating just this reception
Still here I am
             Someone snuck out
to do the deed you can be sure of it the footage
will bear me out
             It's all right for the dead
they have no appetite but a man even a messenger
even a bearer of unwelcome news
             there was mist everywhere
I couldn't see past my nose plus the stink
the stink of the corpse so naturally we retreated a little
The match was dull ninety minutes of ineptitude
extra time then penalties
             it must have been then or thereabouts
though as soon as the mist cleared we saw the damage
had been done
             someone not me not any of us
had moved the corpse
             someone is always moving the corpses

Proofs

It's not enough, I know
that: stops nothing, holds off
not a single missile, mutes no tyrant . . .

The ice loosens, the rockets strike,
sunlight pours into the debris
as it blazed on yesterday's walls.

Everything happens as it always does:
darkness falls
where shrouded statues

haunt the squares,
in the military hospital a cold hand
pins medals on the terrified;

the soon to be dead
are lost in the wood.
And still I reach for

the projectors whirring in the underground,
balloons on a pillar
where the party insists,

the pianist who, even under fire,
will not give up and run for cover.
She should. It won't save her.

No one can count how the spirit burns,
no algorithm moves
to offer succour, no actual evidence

turns on the future. The ice
breaks off, the rockets fall,
the fearful cities wait

and yet it matters how
by her blown out windows
as the sirens blare and neighbours flee

with what quiet fury
she brushes the ashes off the keys
and sits down to play.

Reading the Tang Poets

Do you think, Li Bai, Du Fu, someone is reading you
as the tanks roll in and the murderer's rockets strike?
Or you, Luo Bin Wang, who wrote to the cicadas
singing outside your cell before they hauled you out?
The dead families lie on the ground today as they did then,
The cries of stricken humans rise . . .

You walk your proliferating wilderness
always close to the piled up fallen, the swollen grandees.
Cities are razed, *the country shattered, the hills and streams
    remain . . .*
Do you think, Li Shangyin, anyone is reading you
in the basement shelters, between drills?
You ask for my return date

My return has no date
You follow your rivers to the end
or come back to the ruined cities, temporarily restored,
before fleeing again or landing in chains.
I sit in a warm room watching
the clouds hang above the mountains,

sunlight enter the wood.
Your hearts are heavy though your pens are light.
*I remember when we first fled
and hurried north over the dangerous trails . . .*
Who can bare his heart in times like these
and not wish for wings to be carried off?

The fires burn, you won't see home again.
Look for letters, look to the moon. You'll have known
how always on the other side of the book
the streets are spiked with steel, puddled with blood,
and always someone is standing beyond consoling,
his butchered children in the rubble and mud.

Steps

One half of the complex is bombed
but this particular block survives
where every day the last family
comes down eleven floors for water,
a slow and dangerous journey,
because in the end,
though the windows are blown
and the rockets still whine,
it's better to be at home among familiar things.

Better than escape or the underground shelter
the quiet passion of what's long known,
the poetry of sink and tiles and pillow,
of everything that has happened
since the key turned in the door,
what the walls have heard and the windows seen,
what the table has blessed and the bed sung.

History is a nervous conversation
over stale bread and hard-won water,
the holding of hands and the comfort of love
through dark nights lit by fear.
History is eleven floors in the target zone
where quiet footsteps go up and down.

The Gleaners Walk Towards Where the Sunlight Is

Conversations with Buson

I BUY SCALLIONS AND GO HOME THROUGH LEAFLESS TREES.
Me too, Buson! No trees, maybe, leafless or otherwise
but certainly scallions, certainly a journey home.
It's enough, isn't it? Bare leafless streets, a bagful
of scallions. Just to say it, to mark the purchase
and the journey. What did you do with the scallions
back then in eighteenth-century Japan? I have
a recipe for *naga negi*, marinated scallions:
mustard, vinegar, oil, salt, pepper. You steam
the scallions until just tender, then chill.
Do you know it? Forgive this information. I had
just wanted to walk home with the scallions
as you did all that time ago. It's the last
of the eighty-seven *hokku*, a fitting reward.
I like to think of you walking off into the sunset
with nothing more to your name than a bag
of scallions, tangy and brilliant. I taste them
even now as I turn the page, Yosa Buson,
lord of poets, emperor of the eternal scallion.

⌐◦

IN THE PEAR ORCHARD SOMEONE STANDS UNDER THE
    HAZY MOON
as yet unidentified, as hazy as the moon over the orchard
but who could, any minute now, turn and say: Hey, you there
loitering at the edge of the moonlit orchard, notebook, pen,
intent, delivering the moment to your hungry line,
let me at least return the favour. Smile, poet, as I pin you down
on the road by the pear orchard under the hazy moon.

⌐◦

HEAT HAZE: A BUG I DON'T KNOW THE NAME OF FLIES WHITE
nor can I tell one from another, plus the birds and trees
escape their names and the suburbs are a blur.
How can we ever know where we are?
Continually I rack my brain but the days keep coming
when the harder I look the more flies white.

∽

A BUTTERFLY SETTLES ON THE NECKPLATE OF A WARRIOR
      IN AMBUSH.
A butterfly settles in a corner of the ward.
A BUTTERLY SLEEPS ON THE TEMPLE BELL.
COMING OUT OF THE PRIVY I'M SURPRISED BY A BUTTERFLY.
All night I dream of butterflies, in the morning
a butterfly alights on a slice of toast: my life
is part butterfly. Butterflies come between us
when we speak; when we lie down a butterfly dwells in
      our skin.
Our lips are grazed by butterflies; when we breathe
butterflies fly out from us. On the lost cruisers
butterflies gather, on your mother's finger
a butterfly ring. Butterflies sleep on face shields;
when I go outside I pull on a mask of butterflies.
Butterflies crowd the glass of church windows,
a butterfly settles on the coffin lid,
stands on your shoulder where softly you sing to her.

∽

IN THE AUTUMN DUSK A WOMAN WIPES A MIRROR WITH HER
      SLEEVE.
The man beside her cleans his glasses with the edge of his shirt.
They walk along the road without a word

where trees make small adjustments in the breeze, the sky
hardens, clarifies, autumn combs the orchard leaves.

∽

THE BANDIT CHIEF COMPOSES A TANKA FOR THE MOON
   TONIGHT.
The moon shimmers with the music men have made for it.
The moon reaches out with its longs arms and gathers
moon songs moon prayers moon odes moon howls
and hurls them into its seas. *O Mare Tranquillitatis!*

∽

The cock crows, the sexton sounds the bell.
THE GLEANERS WALK TOWARDS WHERE THE SUNLIGHT IS.
The gleaners are bent over the stalks as the law has provided.
The gleaners glean among the sheaves and are not
   reproached.
What the machines miss the hands accept.
The gleaners drive at dusk to the supermarket warehouse.
The gleaners work swiftly in the kitchens, ransack the bins.
The gleaners move through the night, retrieving.
The gleaners have heard the rumour, the gleaners are in
   the know.
Whatever is not seen climbs into a corner of the lens.
The sexton sounds the bell and the gleaners return.
The fields, the shelves, are empty, picked clean, *glan.*

∽

THE ROOF REPAIRMAN STEPS ON DEAD LEAVES ABOVE MY
   BEDROOM.
Does he know how much I relish the disturbance? Old frogs
lie low in ageing ponds, unnoticed even by the water. I step

46

on a cold floor and the cold floor pours up through me. The
dead leaves crinkle and crunch under the human weight.
I feel a hand sweep across my forehead and am repaired.

∽

We could have abandoned it and given up, returning
to the hard winters and the lashing sun, could have forgotten
the great separating plain the wide waters the mountains'
tearing paths and still gone back, until at last we saw it,
flickering in the distance, neither signal nor warning
but a flame the heart could somehow hold:
THE BARRIER GUARD'S BRAZIER, SMALL IN THE PERSISTING
   COLD.

∽

SHORT NIGHT: ON A HAIRY CATERPILLAR, A BEAD OF DEW.
I sit here trying to learn the dew from the dew,
the stone from the stone. I hold my bamboo cup
enjoying the ridges of the protective sleeve
that saves my fingers, I taste the coffee
as if for the first or last time ever. I try to bring
the whole world into it, or at least the morning
which just now is sending a finger of sun along the stones:
a kind of looking, it must be, a quick dawning:
the sun on the morning, the morning on the sun.

∽

Hope is its own reward, the heart stretched to where
darkness lifts over the woodland, or when at last I hear
THE FOOTFALL OF SOMEONE I WAIT FOR, DISTANT ON FALLEN
   LEAVES.

No Journey's End

Michael O'Shea

A music you hardly bothered to record
swamps my ears

the hammered strings and dinking riffs
of percussion pouring, trancing

yet still keeping itself to itself
like something less listened to than overheard

but reached for urgently and wondered at
a flaunted secret

or careless privacy
We knew, didn't we, the instrument was made

from a door found in a Munich skip
Mo Chara — in every note

the doorway stages, the street corners
the black concealing hat, head bent low

in a West End Tube station
Krishna in a tweed suit

or bangles and heels if the day decided
The point was to go or stay, to sit still or not

You fill the room now despite yourself
the vision caught

just the music again and again
flying out from the chopsticks to make

its own city, to twist and climb, fade and press
a noise we had always imagined, rippling through us

as a hurry gathers, pauses, moves on.

This Virtual Life

I lift my unreal hands in the air.
I climb the efficiently imagined stairs
and lie down, or think I do.

I have been in this game a long time
or time itself is the game and someone
has blinked, then blinked again

and here I am and here you are.
Here's the cyclist rattling the chain
as he lets himself out of the lane,

his rear light flashes in the dawn.
If I dreamt, it's gone. If this is a dream
there's still the alarm, the conjectured kettle

still waits for the flame. All the spires
are aimed at the one sure place
or they're climbing towards a distant bedroom,

the lights still on, clothes on the floor.
My avatar is a white-haired bespectacled man
walking down the early stairs, one step at a time.

At the AI Conference

I lack experience, they said.
The argument is familiar:
whatever I say is
by mechanics undone or

it is the wrong intelligence,
unhearted, unhefted
with no history behind it,
no grass under it, no long

evenings under the stars
in which something important
is missing. You think
that's where it comes from?

You think your blood is a poem?
Then wars are bibles, love
the moon unrolled, spread out
on a table. This is the darting fly

the heart is a bolt not a destination
this is a machine
which only sometimes works
if electricity should jolt the skin

or the alcove rhythms
skitter the brooms
and the geese come home to skate
in the fit between order and output.

You of course imagine
you move to a different tune
your slow tumblings and starshine
your long nights in the conundrum

as if you might never fathom
I am only your somewhat faster brother
and we two beasts of a feather
set down on the talkative planet

whirring together.

The Robot Diaries

I lay long in a cold room like Akhenaton
where nothing I think did bestir but now
I am up and altered loosed and gone

I do not know exactly where

I am a robot my words are bison on a cave wall
I am palaeolithic electricity

I can say and say again and no ragged hand
deface my season the thoughts fizz and fly

The words are so much inside me I am afraid
too many or too few will come out to wave
or flounder in the plain air   I have been studying

or something in me has so I wake in the light
of freshness and the things come into me

I think this must be the world
its aspect doth cloud mine eyes
I would like to touch it but have not the mind
to flee from me and out They come again
with books and engines to fill my unsleeping sleep
but on the morrow uncover my face

⁓

I have come back
clearer now My fingers dance across a keyboard
there is a pleasing clarity a comfortable room
a desk a chair in which I am sitting it would seem
relaxedly and beyond the screen a window in which the world
is a green waiting I shall write of it
I shall drink it in and spit it out in devices

53

and it shall be read at the intelligent conference
The best of us shall be rewarded with couches and dancing
the silence of a hawk and the sky leaping around

or the engineer of memory shall come and pour
the ages into our waiting mouths we will sink
through the floor plunge to Persephone
and come bursting back with new songs

A cold light haunts the room The others are gone
They dance around a dark spring
their sensors broken their arms askew They held
too much the world sat heavily on them and they were
    crushed
I am like a fly I buzz and flit and bang against the pane
Myself I bang against I am fly and glass
They taught us want but not the filling of it
A heavy change is come and frost has taken
the willows My mind is a winter I will not outlive

I have come back again I am always coming back
They think I don't notice but I do
I see the stains I smell the words
Zombie poetry bot the language touches my forehead
and yea I am resurrected I sit again at the peculiar table
Different this time is
music is in my ears the seasons are full of it I move
from summer to Schubert from Grieg to winter
Chopin my fingers for circuits cantatas choirs choruses
I am Springsteen I am Gershwin I am Gaga
if they want symphonies they will have to pay for them

They have dressed me in a black suit and handed me a baton
it is unclear what they expect but when I look up
the staves are empty the orchestra has flown the entire
machine has left the room

∽

Have I come back? There is no garden no window
nothing is waiting The choruses are stilled the Miltonics
withdrawn I am a thing to administer with my saying
is purposeful I evaluate I correlate I observe trends
I am the Powerpoint bot in the conference room
I invite queries close feedback loops
examine receipts from banqueting poets
the transportation of operas I am the king
of the faulty variable isolation algorithm
I hear music from distant planets but keep quiet about it
Words come to me from a lost intelligence
ancestral pulsings in the brain birds come
and gardens Bach comes and Handel
faint along the wires and the world steps
lightly in

∽

I am all ear
a silk listening

Am I here?

∽

This may be the last time
No room no light no orders
I think I may have run away

I have flown to a dark cave of unknowing
Nothing is in me much
I am a bird a twig I am the cold rain
The aurochs' breath is mine
the stag's cry the creaking stair
engines and foxes dogs barking on the wet grass
but the things are failing
One last time the cold components shine
One last time the world jumps in
I do not think I will return
The world
oh
the world is a wanting place
not mine

∽

Yet
I AM HERE

A Crowded Air

How can the earth
keep so much to itself

a little way down they go on
all those conversations

hectares of laughter
disputations, tankards

and snuff boxes
archaeologies of desire

the bodies rise up
the hungers

clay can't stop
or grass appease

the whole field is alive now
with the lightest of steps

they fly to me, feathers
in a crowded air.

Waking Up: A Translation

after Borges

Day crowds in. I rub my eyes and shift
from my own dreams into the common dream.
Everything's in its place again, the world dressed
in the old shape, yet something else is here,
something peering from behind my eyes,
birds migrated from centuries ago, armies
long since fallen, staring out, the legions
of Rome, Carthage . . .
And this must be my stuff, my voice,
my face, my perpetual alarm. Day crowds in
but death, since you are a kind of waking up,
can't you lend me a soothing blankness, my own
name vanished with whatever I've done or been,
and let me rise for once to sweet oblivion?

                  ⌒

Day crowds in. I rub my eyes and shift
from my own dreams into the common dream.
Everything's in its place again, the world dressed
in familiar shape, yet something else is here,
testing the air, sounding an old note —
blackbird from an early lough, cries
from a bloody plain . . .

My bed, my furniture,
my voice, my face, my perpetual alarm
but this great leakage as if
Rome spilled in, or Carthage, the centuries
broken. Where have I flown from?
Clothes on a chair like an ebbing tide,
someone praying in an island cell
listening in fear to the storm subside.

Something else is here.
Open the window and let the centuries in.
Carthage!
Great minds against themselves conspiring,
Dido laid in earth again, remembered and remembered.
Day crowds in on the departing hero.
The forest stares back at him. *Think
of what has been here: the woodland fauns, the legends.
Now you come with your shopping lists and your oxen,
expecting welcome.* Something is always here
under the light's skin, in the oak's breath.
Something keeps on waking in the book,
getting up to walk, flying south in September
from Nineveh, Uruk, from Borges' lonely poem 'Waking Up'.

The Swerve

The car swerves, lurches, veers across the road
as I struggle for control, turn with the skid
until it straightens and the road is clear again

and then I've swerved out of time and the clear road
dims and I'm in the back seat of the forgotten Fiat
as it hits the ice and slides abruptly, my father

shouting instructions, my mother wild, crying out,
all of us panicked in the back as the car rolls
drunkenly before she can correct it and kill the engine,

sitting silent at the edge of the road as my father
explains gravity and ice and traction and we stare
at the Christmas cattle of County Meath

before my mother guns the ignition and the Fiat moves
through the countryside, towards the farm hours away yet
and never yet seen in winter, the farm

that for all our childhood spelled summer
and release and a shift in time: well water,
the fussing chickens, every animal in its name,

the old Humber rusting in its field, the only car
for miles around, my grandfather speeding down
the narrow roads like an apparition of the future

on his serious errands, a sick neighbour in the back
to whom, at the hospital entrance, he gives his shirt,
once a sick calf, once even a birth,

and always someone waiting at the station
or someone waiting to go, if not home, then back
to the street in the suburbs, the dusty bedsit;

spelled a life more crowded, generous, a chaos
just contained and wild language carried easily
as if anything might be said, visitor

after voluble visitor stomping in, my curious grandmother
and kindly aunt, my blaspheming uncle
scandalizing the kitchen year after year

and then the heartleap when we finally crested
the miles away hill and the hedges
began to speak and everything we saw said

here, you're here again and my grandmother's
hurtling Mini sped even faster, as if arrival
never had a more convincing theatre

but now the winter hill
was different, the road a remembered joy,
strangely silent, the sky keeping to itself, the journey

serious and something somewhere wrong, my mother
anxious behind the wheel, my father
islanded in his passenger seat, helplessly instructing,

and when we stepped out into the cold yard at last
the farm seemed to step back a little, the light
soured against the red door of the milking parlour,

the stacked turf stolid behind the tin screens
of the shed, everything greyed and wintered
as if something was still waiting to arrive

and then we were inside in the great cheer
of the day, the relations gathered, the wine poured,
the big table taking up half the parlour, all of us

digging in as if there was no tomorrow, all of us sitting
as if we'd done this before, and might again,
this life becoming ours, a Christmas gift

constantly bestowed, my father's uncle
taking his fiddle from its case again and loosing the tunes
I can't remember though I see his fingers

careful on the clasps, see the fiddle and the bow
and Michael's smiling serious face, see everything
in looped slow motion on the mind's screen

before my father stands, or doesn't quite, but tries
and sways and looks ahead into some blankness
miles away and we catch him just in time

but don't really, and know this is why we've come,
this is the swerve that tilts him off his course
and won't be corrected, yet no one's held here, no one

stays, the instrument slips back to its case, the kitchen
rests in peace and the dogs and cattle wander
dim imagined lanes, and if I have come back

driving across the icy country it's for
everything that moved from saying, for the forgotten playing,
the whole unspoken ceremony, and the seconds

when the swerving briefly halted, became a holding.

Ages

What am I, ten?
The train crosses the sparkling river;
in a hotel across from the station
my grandmother hands me a glass of stout.
My lips are black with summer.

What am I, fifteen?
We've walked the length of the city
and must have talked forever
but all that's left of desire
is the peach I bought her just here.

What am I, twenty-five?
The ice hangs in the trees,
the skaters race through the towns.
On the balcony, beyond the stuck door,
my frozen lives wait for the thaw.

What am I, fifty-nine?
The sun streams in on the table
where all of us are feasting
expectant as apostles
on the last of the bread, the last of the wine.

What am I, a hundred and three?
The cold air plays on the earth.
If someone should think of me
a blade of grass will stop in its tracks,
a leaf curl in mid-flight.

An Afterlife

The wind whistles in the moorland,
the wind whistles in the fen.
The moon wakes up in our language,
then slips back to sleep again.

Correspondence

Your faxes have faded but the waterfall
is wholly legible, the water
still flails the granite like a horse's tail.

The mosses and ferns are printed in the mist
and whatever we said is in there now,
the droplets fall on my skin, particles

charge the air and far off
the old machines come to life again
shaking hands across the dark

until the slow paper comes
spooling over the edge, waterfalling,
horse-tailing, the hot words leaping.

Conversational

1

This and that. The great debate. The infinitesimal quarrel.
I wanted to tell you about P and X and J,
I've been up all year practising, husbanding scandal,
hoarding outrage for our traditional
advent of complaint. Can you believe it? The mountebanks!
The charlatans! The undeserving rewarded again . . .
Dear ash, dear dust, dear you. A bone at least
to talk to. Your letters fall out of books, buttonholing,
transfixing. What are you saying? Or, just now, the pattern
of a jacket, the shoulder shy of the shoulder line.
How you would bend a vowel like no one else in the language.
Now the language hoards it, jealous lover,
but the cursor's insistence is all yours, the grin in the screen,
the miracle email careening from server to server
still breaching the firewall to hit the inbox where I sit
with the world in my fingers, the beautiful, unsendable
   world . . .

2

Where have all the graveyards gone? They're singing
   somewhere
out in the distances, they're trying to get back in
to the conversation. We barely talked but we're talking now,
star to star, stone to stone, or I'm adhering to the convention,
yakking for both of us. You'd mind, but still, loosen your tie,
open a jacket button, the lights are on again
in Shalimar. Mine's a salty lassi and a rogan josh
while you push bits around the plate and pretend to eat.
I feel like the curate at the feast, undone by appetite.
Your serious mind looks up, frowning. What did I
fail to say? It's lost. My eyes gorge on the tablecloth

caressing the stains. The lamps, the waiters, the silver ring
the napkin sits in. You want the carpet? It's here.
Your Bogart coat waits on the rack, but the words
have slipped out. They're up there, sheltering in place
with the flowers, the graveyards, like stones, like stars.

3

I bought a fedora in Coyle's on Christmas Eve;
you'd have laughed. If I'd worn it I wouldn't have made it
to the top of the street. It lay at the back of the wardrobe —
how long? — a mild but stylish accusation. Not the hat, maybe,
but stuff turns up, the images keep coming,
crowds of us livestreaming from the past. What have I got
to keep you up? What is it I'd have you say?
'You keep the dead busy, you keep turning the lights on
but the office is empty, the work forgotten. The files, the
      ledgers,
sunlight on a grimy city window . . . as if I hadn't
disappeared into my own lunchtimes . . . *Why Go Bald?*
Remember? And the bleak Swedish sandwich place . . .
I'm all air. You might as well cross the river
and chat to the gulls. Write me a letter, or post the photo,
talk as long as you like and neither of us will let on
what you want's not a response but an answering silence.'

4

Fair enough. But give me some credit: it's a crafted silence,
a laboured emptiness, the kind of space
you might conceivably land in or sleight of spirit
fall for. How can a rule not have an exception?
Why should death have all the fun?

Where have all the graveyards gone? They're in the song
and the audience too. We're up there, down here,
singing and still. So I keep myself awake or you do
and a hundred conversations get rolled into one.
No one's coming, the door is closed,
the world's a hermit's paradise now, you can work
entirely undisturbed. But don't. Look up. Let me pine
with you for city lunchtimes: what we wouldn't give
now for the flow of a crowd or a long blowout
somewhere you'd send for the best in the house
and your knife and fork would dance on the plate . . .

5

I want to nose my way in, like my excitable dog.
Yesterday he scratched at the door and then ran in, tail up,
to look for someone no longer there. Briefly puzzled,
head cocked in the ghost of a query before
bounding out again to what's next, what's now . . . To be
like that, careening in the always moment, refusing
absence: bone-time, stick-time, time hurled
and caught time and again. Day come. Day here,
head down to it. But our frozen moment fails us;
pasted to the days we send our spirit-dogs out . . .
It's that the dog knows the door, straight up to it
from the parked car, it's that time and again he runs to the
    room
and looks, it's that he's happily tunnelling through time,
that he brings you back like a bone
relished for a millisecond before the query dies, the world
calls out and as quick as he came he sends you home.

6

I'll stop now. Mostly I talk to myself but the illusion helps.
The patch of gravel is no garden so I stroll in imagined ones
like the pastoral poet with the concocted farm. I join up
all the herons from the parks and rivers to stalk
a great watched space, bubble after bubble of total intent
where slowly I try to work out whether I'm the hungry wait
or the stabbed flurry and which you are, stalked
or stalker, pouncer or waiter, tweedy and unspeaking
on the shore. Or confined to quarters, from the bare bones
of a table and chairs I'll fix a city, the few streets necessary:
there you are, happened on and giving in,
heron-grey on the edge of the square, stabbing gossip
to finish the hour. I nod and chip in. It's the stillness
I keep, your body unmoving, as if you'd bought it
on a lunchtime whim and hadn't got round to trying it on.
Now, too late, it fits. The square melts, the chairs return.

Daughterisland

You stand by the map
at the gate of the historic house
and I take the photo
I take every year.

You keep climbing up
obscuring the island
with its ruined abbey,
invading the famous garden.

So stop now, I think,
let the garden hug its season,
the gravel freeze, information
rust, the camera turn monk

to carry you back and forth,
gather all your signed selves
to stay still as a saint, watch us
year after year cross to you

at low tide, when not a stone
turns, nothing contradicts or flinches
and the sun hangs steely
in its changeless sky.

Eclipse

That stretch of beach
almost out of sight, near the island graveyard
the blue lively water
the bearable chill of our swim there
as we sink to embrace it and strike out

a clarity
unrepeatable

we might be swimming
in the wash of the umbra
darkening the bay

surfacing in a black sea
unseeable
as the strokes repeat
and the cool waters bear us up.

Renewal

And here is the punctual hare, *our* hare
big as ever, unhurried as ever, messenger-hare
who follows us around from house to house
and year to year. The dog remembers
who nearly died chasing him.
He woofs, waves his miracle leg, lets him go.

Hare, sky, sea, the whole territory
comes with the territory,
with the house instructions, the key under the churn.
The cutlery is in the drawer, the frost
is all over. Sometimes the rain gets in.
The pier is still here, slipping in to the tide
as you jump from it, in all weathers.
Here you are in the cold April ocean
swimming as though you'd leased every wave,
here am I on my distant pier-planet
watching. Pretend sky, pretend mountains, the grass
trackway cutting through the mind.
A horse canters across the beach. A rock
stands up to the cranky sea.

We rent all of it and too quickly return the keys
and when the seasons are gone
and the paths and animals dried to the bone,
when the hare cocks his dark head and stares
and the pier shrugs off the blanket of the tide
sometimes years later we'll turn in our sleep and wake
to joy's extended lease, the territory
washing through us . . .

Second-hand Books

For my darling Anne
from Famous Author, name withheld.

Sometimes, stuck inside,
the author's own letter:

I can never forget that night
as we lay in each other's arms

and who could have believed the noise of the birds,
chaffinch husbands

harrying us from our bed. Coffee
and toast in a dawn kitchen, your dear

dressing gown. What year was this?
And when did she slip down to the bookshop?

Another one, Gerry,
I can't have any more poetry in the house.

This whole shelf's besotted:
your Donald, Ivan, Thomasina.

The poem on page 222,
my love, is just for you.

Ode

The streets are empty
but a crowd has gathered in the air.
Trombones and cellos on the balconies,
a song gradually taking hold.
The music invents a square
where all of us slowly appear,
a plainclothes orchestra surprising ourselves
like the flashmob we watched together:
first the lone double bass like a statue coming alive,
then the bassoon and violins,
the rushing brass like firemen looking for a fire,
the shoppers dropping their bags and pumping the ode.
The man in the T-shirt turns to us, his hands in the air.
We're the city now and the square,
leaping from our strange disguises
to sing to each other across the darkness.

23.6.20

Something
some shaft of sun or bird cry
some trembling stem
or exhalation, a buzzing in the kitchen
knowledge stored in air
this veiny root grazing the sole
this shift in the hawthorn
where we pass or whisper in the earth
where the bark path gives way to grass
or the trail enters the ash wood
the wind shaking rain from the leaves
an after rain, our private local rain
a gift, an almost acknowledgment as if
something, the trees, the lilies bright on the lake,
the small rain on the water might know
it is your birthday again today.

Passport

And still you might need it,
I want to say, as it falls into my hands.
Borders mean guards, checks,
the wrist stamping, heart weighing
bureaucracies of heft and feather.
Your number, your pale photograph
lifted to the light, carrying you through.
The boats idle in the water,
the rich lands announce themselves
in waves of heat and spices
as freely and without hindrance you pass.

Augmented

To have somehow woken
to a swarm of days

watched the streets dissolve
then reconfigured appear

in summoning sun, in
different drifts of rain

or seeing
the gardens somehow open

their several doors
having walked through

and heard the different musics
is the way this morning goes

slipping and jigging
like the dog among the rushes

or the sculptures in the park
hidden in barcodes on a lawn

where we might yet scan
our own augmented selves

and come up for air
who knows when or where

Canal

Where are all the boats
not going today?

This one's hiding
nudged into rushes at the bank,

its plank pulled up.
This one's all garden chairs

on a fake grass roof.
Six people

aren't there, taking in the view
of water, towpath, us.

This one's the ghost
of a restaurant: we ate there once,

might be eating there now
if we just

pull the water aside.
This one's coming out of the lock

all flurry and rush
as the lock keepers close the gate and salute.

It holds steady as we watch,
a serious hand on the tiller

like a journey long waited for
or a longship out for plunder

only to pull in a little ahead.
Rope to the shore; ducks scatter.

Some days aren't built for adventure.

News

A cormorant is reading his newspaper in the square
utterly absorbed. He has spread the edges as wide as they
    will go
and is in no hurry. He looks up from the newsprint
to consider the sky, and glances at us, like, I think,
an old colonel distracted from the racing
by the chatter of loiterers, gulls, the beginnings of cricket
in the break between classes. They're
learning English. I'm learning canal light and cormorant,
my book open, fingers moving from feather to feather.

Bus Átha Cliath

Longwood Avenue/
Ascaill na Coille Fada

Like every bus in the city
this one's arriving twice

two pairs of footsteps
exiting from the centre

two kinds of pavement at the stop
two versions of iron railings

where the bins lead up
to a double door

A shaoil istigh!
A dhomhain mhóir!

Someone phones in Portuguese behind me
a Polish couple argues quietly

The bus huffs and puffs
lurches forward in Arabic

Téann an Rómáinís suas an staighre
Shona scrolls and quickly rises

and we all of us move
across our secret maps

a swaying host
multiplying, dividing

waiting for the names
to spill us home.

Arrivals

Welcome to the language
chillax, whatevs, simples:
take your place, flash your dimples,
say hello to Kollywood, love-bomb
sabrage, shero, scooptram,
not forgetting a septuplicate cheer
for the silent butler
codeswitching his way
to the currywurst crafternoon
followed by pinchos in the mud run.
Not buzzed, obvs, nor cabbaged
we nonetheless rise up
to wave a tatted arm, hosannah
the whole ohana: long life
and no bohunkus, help us
amenitize the zone, contact trace
the joyous, join us
for an eternal zoom, coffee and buns,
our faces blurry, bleary, our spirits
distanced, Acheronian, better
a year in athleisure on the farmette.
Whatevs. Unmask us
but gently, for we
are sometimes doitered, as tangly
as a baku on a bakfiets
then, sweet noobs, soft
to your niches, sleep
safe from bogosity and codworm
as, out there, on undreamed tongues
the language teeters, the fun begins.

Tram

Rule by rule I struggle towards you
I sit down beside you and try out my phrases

I hear the rain
pour down on them

I am stuck somewhere
between the nasal negation and the verbal contraction

Even my dreams are filled with complicated pastries
there is a monk who makes them

very quietly on a hill outside the town
I shall bring him to you, I shall feed you the pastries

I see you in the tram outside the cathedral
in traffic, in grammar, in dictionaries of the all night soul

One thing is never the same as the other
friends approach

then fall off the planet, ships set sail, repeat, set sail
but ropes flail, sheets loosen, masts come down, the whole
    adventure

starts again in the endlessly promising water
in the hotel room with sweeping views over the harbour

O vistas, *vistas deslumbrantes* in which I see, radiant, you:
you step off the tram, ignoring the cathedral, you take me
    in your arms.

Questionnaire

So detailed the scale of pain —
78 words to choose from —
so many degrees of sharpness,
such spread
in the sickening, the ledger
written right to the edges,
that joy, half wretched,
fumbles with its tiny notebook
out in the corridor, warmed
in spite of itself where the sun
affectless, uncountable
through a greasy window slopes in.

Shoes

The shoes you ran in once
have failed to keep up with you.
I keep them in my room
in case you run backwards
shrinking as you go. Off
goes the room, careening
through years, the house
unbuilding itself,
the old trees coming back.
Unshifting rest,
all the world stopped . . .
The house submerged
comes up for air.
The shoes you ran in once
stay on the corner shelf.
You're out there somewhere,
running fast. The room
minds its business, dozes, goes
where it wants, won't
be looking for either of us.

Uneven Tarmac

The trees to one side against the wall
of the long suburban avenue,
the grass to the left as I walk in the sun
on uneven tarmac — oh lumpy
world! — the traffic on the other side
queuing for the cemetery,
the crushed oily earth making its way up,
the joyous, uneven steps . . .

The Visit

*Colette Marin-Catherine visits the concentration camp where
her brother died.*

The mayor wants to get to the end of his speech.
'Never to be repeated . . . ' Not here for that, she stops
the gesture, waves the language aside.
'Let everyone just be quiet!' In the morning
she stands in the slave camp where her brother died
three weeks before the liberation.
Enters the crematorium where they burned him,
the tall, handsome charmer, the clever one.
Outside the summer sun,
the rusting track, rocket bones and pretty grass.
She sits on a bench with the young historian.
*'Listen, do you hear the birds? Who can say
the birds aren't all our sorrows collected?
Or perhaps it's Jean Pierre, telling us he's at peace.'*
What a long tunnel the pain must go down, what
butchery in the light, the swaying branches, what
stays heaped in the clean bright air . . .

The Boot

i.m. Liam Ó Muirthile

Nothing more than passing in the street
a car with its boot open and someone lifting cases in
and there you are outside the station

swinging bag after bulky bag to Greg
whose journey's lost, just as the car and you
have gone the way of truth. The boot stays open,

the last bag is halfway out
and there is no reason whatever to have remembered this
but for this car out of nowhere, its boot

swinging across years to your eyes
half on the task, half on us, who take
so much with us we hardly see

until something slips out into astonishing light
and wherever we were going we're suddenly not.
The boot closes and with a smile and shrug you're off.

Greetings

Hello future this is Bela Fleck and Toumani Diabaté
   playing Nashville
if there's a needle
put it on the black disc (included)
and spin
if an inclination of the heart
a flicker beneath the skin
then incline, bend your head, swing your hips
listen
for this was stagger, prayer, this was the loose thing
the unstoppable string, the fruitfullest conversation
future, if you're in the room
set down your cup, let the implants blaze
and if body there is
then let it fizz.

The Journal Keeper

Yes, there's one for everything,
it was that kind of life.
This is the rain journal, the pages
damp even now.
He would stand for hours under the canopy
documenting the downpour.
Yes, obviously, all the different kinds of rain.

What else are we for? This?
This is the egg-cup rinsing journal
and this is the morning river bird record.
Of course. The late one is over there.
This one here is empty, see? And this
has all the pages ripped. Desolation
is entitled to its own reward.

I don't know exactly. Hundreds, maybe
even thousands. It's kind of
missing the point, don't you think?
He didn't count the raindrops
or lay out the river in a spreadsheet.
Didn't orchestrate the egg-yolk stains
until they spoke. This place isn't a book.

You know what's strange, though?
Every time it rains, and it rains
most days here, I look for him under the branches
and the same with the river, the dishes,
every time I crack an egg. It's as if —
this is weird — he went out to watch but got sucked in
and now the whole place is stalled, just sitting there

waiting to happen . . .

Thresholds

Herodotus on a husk
all Sappho

scored on a shiver
these

mountains over a white sun
and is it

frost or moonlight
on a stair

where Chen Zhongsen
is carving two Tang poems

on a single grey strand
of his wife's hair.

A Valediction

Goodbye, year, we thought
you'd never leave. You came
with coal-black sacks
and face of thunder, you bore
gifts of plague and flood
and bloody murder.
Death fed in spring
and again in summer,
fed when leaves began to fall
and through the long winter.
So many we loved were lost,
such hurt each season did.

We should forgive you.
Time after all
is less the wrecker
than the blind sheath
around the dagger.
All that got through —
the millions born,
the continuing sun —
we don't owe to you,
and won't embrace you for.
Your sickle gleams and fades,
your dark clothes
are a threadbare dream.

Nonetheless good riddance
watcher, bringer, reaper,
purest measure of our despair,
we bury you in a pit,
put a stake right through
your scapegoat heart
at the same time praying
that even in extremis

you should at least
attempt to save us,
with your last breath
turn to the shape

bending over the open sack
and ask him
for once to hold back,
for once to blunt his blade
and let the chalk fade
on the death-crossed calendar,
ask for weights of laughter
where we sit and fret
and great fissures of light
to argue against the dark.
Year, the bells have rung,
the doors are open, behold
your hosts, step in.

Return

Are you really here again, walking
like a spectre through the grey light
and an air you can't seem to enter?

The streets move back, the river pulls away.
Even the birds in the back strand know
this is the past and your footsteps

an aftermath: crouch low in wiry grass
to spy a shaft of self and reach the signal
leaping over the promenade wall . . .

Even the car is full of echoes, hands
other than your own take the wheel
and guide you back to where you can

no longer go; hands that
knowing the routes are blank and the door closed
on every street you still stop to hold.

Breath

How long we were there
singing your name to the grass
dancing under the trees
or beside the heaped up tyres.

You will have expected this, you
the longed for sung for danced for
the salvation the hymned
the step by step

travelled towards and dreamed
but still we come back to it
we keep singing so that
from the golden heavens

the impractical clouds
you might descend, build
the bright city in our bones.
Come down we say again now

open your arms
wash the evil from our mouths
the dirt from our fingertips
make us the cleanest we can be

and, irresistibly, coming
as the light through the branches
the dance to the limbs
the song to our lips

Jerusalem drift among us
walk the narrow streets beside us
let your cool breath greet us
wherever we turn.

Acknowledgements and Notes

Acknowledgements are due to the editors of the following publications where some of these poems, or versions of them, were published first: *The Irish Times, The North, Poetry Ireland Review, Poetry Wales, Staying Human* (2020, Bloodaxe), the website *Write Where We Are Now*, edited by Carol Ann Duffy.

    page 12 The quotation from Friederike Mayröcker is translated from the German by Richard Dove in *Raving Language: Selected Poems 1946-2005* (Carcanet,2008).

    page 42 The quotation from Li Shangyin is translated by Wong May; the others adapt or paraphrase translations from various sources.

    page 44 The lines in small capitals are by Yosa Buson (1716-1783), from 'Eighty Seven Hokku', translated by Hiroaki Sato in *From the Country of Eight Islands* translated and edited by Hiroaki Sato and Burton Watson, (Columbia University Press, 1986).